THE VERY BEST BOOK

Written by **CHRISTY WEIR** • Illustrated by **NAN BROOKS**

With love to my kids, Erin and Jeremy.

Library of Congress Cataloging-in-Publication Data
Weir, Christy.
The very best book : the story of the Dead Sea Scrolls and the Bible /
Christy Weir, author; Nan Brooks, illustrator.
p. cm. Summary: Briefly describes how the Dead Sea Scrolls were found and
their relationship to the book we know as the Bible.
ISBN 0-8307-1595-9
1. Dead Sea Scrolls—Juvenile literature. 2. Bible—Juvenile literature.
[1. Dead Sea Scrolls. 2. Bible.] I. Brooks, Nan, ill. II. Title.
BM487.W44 1993 296.1′55—dc20 92-32744 CIP AC

Rights for publishing this book in other languages are contracted by Gospel Literature
International (GLINT). GLINT also provides technical help for the adaptation,
translation, and publishing of Bible study resources and books in scores of
languages worldwide. For further information, contact GLINT, Post Office
Box 488, Rosemead, California, 91770, U.S.A., or the publisher.

Regal Books
A Division of Gospel Light
Ventura, California 93006
Printed in U.S.A.

THE DEAD SEA SCROLLS

In 1947 an important discovery was made in the rocky desert west of the Dead Sea. Stories of the discovery vary in detail, so historians may never determine precisely what happened. The most common story tells of an Arab shepherd boy named Mohammed-ad-Dhib who was tending his goats on the hillsides near Qumran. When a runaway goat entered a cave in a nearby cliff face, Mohammed threw a stone inside and heard a strange noise. He had broken a clay jar. Mohammed explored the cave and found several jars about two feet tall containing leather scrolls wrapped in linen. Mohammed didn't know it at the time, but he had found a manuscript of the book of Isaiah written 2,000 years ago.

In the following years, Bedouins and archaeologists continued the search for manuscripts, discovering fragments of more than 400 scrolls hidden in 11 caves. Using paleography (the study of deciphering ancient writings), archaeology (the study of physical evidence, such as potsherds, fragments of cloth and coins found in the caves) and Carbon 14 dating, the scrolls have been found to originate around A.D. 33, plus or minus 100 years. One theory states that the scrolls were part of a library belonging to a Jewish religious sect living at Khirbet Qumran during the time of Jesus. Their scrolls were quickly packed up and stored away for safekeeping in nearby caves when the Roman army reconquered Palestine in putting down the great revolt of A.D. 66-70.

The Dead Sea Scrolls contain copies of every one of the books of the Old Testament except Esther. They are a thousand years older than any previously known surviving Bible manuscript and show very few changes in content or wording over the past 20 centuries. Bible scholars have been amazed at the accuracy with which scribes copied the manuscripts through the years. They feel confident that what we read in our Bible today is the same message God gave to its writers long ago.

Want to find out more about the very best Book? You can read these verses in your Bible.
About the Bible—_Psalm 119:9-11,105; 2 Timothy 3:16; Hebrews 4:12_
About Creation—_Genesis 1 and 2_
About Moses and the Ten Commandments—_Exodus 19:20—20:22_
About poems and songs—_Psalms_
About Jesus—_Matthew 4:23-25; Mark 10:13-16; 15; 16; Luke 22:70,71_

One little goat was missing.
Where could it be?
Mohammed looked across the hot,
rocky desert. He saw his herd of goats.
He counted again.
Yes—one goat was gone.

Mohammed kicked a rock. "I'm their shepherd,"
he thought. "I've got to find that lost goat."

Kerplunk. What was that? Kerplunk!
A shower of pebbles fell down a steep cliff.

Mohammed squinted his eyes and looked up. He saw a cave way up high on the cliff. More pebbles fell at his feet.

"Maybe that's where my little goat is!" said Mohammed.
He picked up a pebble. "This pebble will chase him out
of the cave," thought Mohammed.

Mohammed aimed the pebble. It sailed through the air.
Higher and higher. Clunk! It missed the cave.
Mohammed picked up another pebble and threw again.

Into the cave it flew! Crack!
"What was that?" wondered Mohammed. It wasn't a goat.
It sounded like something breaking. What could be in that cave?

Up, up Mohammed quickly climbed.
Over a hill, over rocks, all the way to
the top of the cliff.

Mohammed stopped to take a deep breath.
Then he moved toward the cave. What was inside?

Mohammed looked in.
It was cool in the cave, and too dark to see.

Mohammed stood very still. The cave smelled old and musty. Then, "m-a-a-a-a, m-a-a-a-a"—a soft sound came from the back of the cave. "My goat!" said Mohammed. That smart little goat had gone into the cave looking for a cool, shady place to rest.

Mohammed stepped toward the goat. Klunk!
He tripped over something hard. It was a big, clay jar.
So that's what his pebble had hit. But wait!
The jar was broken and there was something inside!

Very, very carefully, Mohammed reached inside the jar.
Very, very carefully, he pulled something out.
It looked like a roll of paper! A scroll!

The scroll was very, very old.
And there was writing on the scroll—
writing that Mohammed couldn't read.

What a discovery! Mohammed could hardly believe it!
He was holding a scroll that was older than his grandfather.
Older than his grandfather's grandfather! He had to tell someone.
He had to find out what was written on the old, old scroll.

Do you know what was written on the scroll?
The writing was words of a very old book.
An ancient book. The best book in the whole world.
And that book is...the Bible!

There are lots and lots and lots of books.
Millions and billions. There are storybooks,
songbooks, silly books, sad books.
Why is the Bible the very best book of all?

The Bible is a gift God gave to you.
Because you're special. Because He loves you.
The Bible tells all about God's love.

The Bible has 66 books inside.
And 40 people wrote them.
A fisherman, a king, a doctor, and many more.

It took a long time for those people to write the Bible. They didn't have typewriters and computers and printers. Sometimes they wrote on scrolls made of goat or sheep skin. They called this parchment. Sometimes they wrote with a sharp stick on wax tablets. Other times they wrote on pieces of broken pottery.

The Bible is full of stories, poems and songs.
Not pretend stories. All the stories in the Bible are true.
They really happened!

The first book in the Bible is called Genesis.
Genesis means "beginning." Do you know what happened
in the very beginning? The Bible says God made the world.
Then He made all the plants and all the animals.
The world was perfect!

But what was missing? People!
So God made a man and a woman.
God loved Adam and Eve and they loved God, too.
Together they took good care of the earth God made.

Many years went by. Now lots of people lived on the earth.
Some people loved God. But other people forgot about God.
They became selfish and angry.

God still loved the people. He wanted them to be happy and do what is right. So God gave some very special laws to a man named Moses. Do you know what the laws are called? The Ten Commandments. God wants all people to obey His commands.

The greatest story in all the Bible begins when a special
baby was born. Do you know His name?
The baby's name was Jesus and He is God's Son.
Jesus grew and grew, just like you.

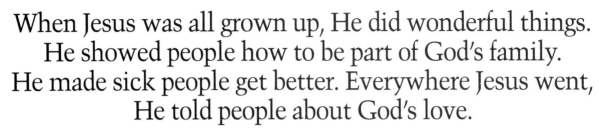

When Jesus was all grown up, He did wonderful things.
He showed people how to be part of God's family.
He made sick people get better. Everywhere Jesus went,
He told people about God's love.

The Bible tells that Jesus loved children.
He was their good friend.
Jesus loves you, too. He will be your good friend.
He will care for you always.

The Bible is more than just a book.
It is God's Word, written especially for you and me.
The Bible is an amazing book.
A forever book. God's "I love you" book.
That's why the Bible is the very best book.